Athena

BY VIRGINIA LOH-HAGAN

Gods and goddesses were the main characters of myths. Myths are traditional stories from ancient cultures. Storytellers answered questions about the world by creating exciting explanations. People thought myths were true. Myths explained the unexplainable. They helped people make sense of human behavior and nature. Today, we use science to explain the world. But people still love myths. Myths may not be literally true. But they have meaning. They tell us something about our history and culture.

45th Parallel Press

Published in the United States of America by Cherry Lake Publishing
Ann Arbor, Michigan
www.cherrylakepublishing.com

Content Adviser: Matthew Wellenbach, Catholic Memorial School, West Roxbury, MA
Reading Adviser: Marla Conn MS, Ed., Literacy specialist, Read-Ability, Inc.
Book Designer: Jen Wahi

Photo Credits: © Lisa S./Shutterstock.com, 5; © v0v/canstockphoto.com, 6; © Susana Guzmán Martínez, 8; © Cromagnon, 11; © johnrochaphoto/Austria/Alamy Stock Photo, 13; © North Wind Picture Archives/Alamy Stock Photo, 15; © Chronicle/Alamy Stock Photo, 17; © muratart/Shutterstock.com, 19; © Gilmanshin/Shutterstock.com, 21; © milosk50/Shutterstock.com, 22; © Howard David Johnson, 2016, 25; © Elle Arden Images/Shutterstock.com, 27; © Ammit Jack/Shutterstock.com, 29; © Howard David Johnson, 2016, Cover; various art elements throughout, shutterstock.com

45th Parallel Press is an imprint of Cherry Lake Publishing.

Library of Congress Cataloging-in-Publication Data

Names: Loh-Hagan, Virginia, author.
Title: Athena / by Virginia Loh-Hagan.
Description: Ann Arbor : Cherry Lake Publishing, [2017] | Series: Gods and
  goddesses of the ancient world | Includes bibliographical references and
  index.
Identifiers: LCCN 2016031219| ISBN 9781634721356 (hardcover) | ISBN
  9781634722674 (pbk.) | ISBN 9781634722018 (pdf) | ISBN 9781634723336
  (ebook)
Subjects: LCSH: Athena (Greek deity)--Juvenile literature. | Goddesses,
  Greek--Juvenile literature. | Mythology, Greek--Juvenile literature.
Classification: LCC BL820.M6 L65 2017 | DDC 292.2/114--dc23
LC record available at https://lccn.loc.gov/2016031219

Printed in the United States of America
Corporate Graphics

ABOUT THE AUTHOR:

Dr. Virginia Loh-Hagan is an author, university professor, former classroom teacher, and curriculum designer. She strives to be wiser. She reads a lot of books and watches a lot of documentaries. She lives in San Diego with her very tall husband and very naughty dogs. To learn more about her, visit www.virginialoh.com.

TABLE OF CONTENTS

ABOUT THE AUTHOR 2

CHAPTER 1:
WARRIOR GODDESS 4

CHAPTER 2:
WISDOM AND WARS 10

CHAPTER 3:
CRUEL AND UNUSUAL PUNISHMENTS 16

CHAPTER 4:
BATTLE GEAR 20

CHAPTER 5:
HELP FROM ATHENA 26

DID YOU KNOW? 30
CONSIDER THIS! 31
LEARN MORE 31
GLOSSARY 32
INDEX 32

WARRIOR GODDESS

Who is Athena? How was she born? What other names does Athena have?

Athena was a Greek goddess. She was one of the 12 **Olympians**. These gods ruled over all of the gods. They lived on Mount Olympus. Mount Olympus is in Greece. It's the highest mountain in Greece.

Athena's father was Zeus. Zeus was the god of the sky. He was the king of gods. Zeus married a **Titan** named Metis. Titans are giant gods. Metis was the mother of wisdom and deep thought. She became pregnant. A goddess told Zeus that their child would kill him. So, Zeus turned Metis into a fly. He swallowed her. He didn't want her to give birth.

Metis continued to live. She lived inside of Zeus's head. She made her baby a robe. She made her baby a helmet. She hammered. This gave Zeus a headache.

Zeus was in pain. He wanted it to stop. Another god used a golden ax. He split Zeus's head open. Out came Athena. She was born as an adult. She was born dressed like a warrior.

Athena was born into power.

Athena and Triton were cousins.

She was born to fight.

Athena was Zeus's favorite daughter. She was an independent woman. She never married. She didn't have lovers. She didn't have children.

Athena had a best friend. Her name was Pallas. Pallas was Triton's daughter. Triton was a sea god. Athena and Pallas did everything together. They practiced their fighting skills. One day, they had a real fight. Pallas was about to strike

Athena. Zeus stepped in. He stunned Pallas. Athena hit Pallas. She didn't mean to do it. She wounded her. Pallas died.

Family Tree

Grandparents: Cronus (god of time) and Rhea (goddess of fertility)

Parents: Zeus (god of the sky), Metis (mother of wisdom and deep thought)

Half-brothers: Ares (god of war), Hephaestus (god of fire and craftsmen), Apollo (god of music), Hermes (messenger of the gods), Dionysus (god of wine), Heracles (Greek hero), Minos (king of Crete), Perseus (Greek hero)

Half-sisters: Eris (goddess of strife), Eileithyia (goddess of childbirth), Enyo (goddess of war), Hebe (goddess of youth), Artemis (goddess of the hunt), Aphrodite (goddess of love), the Muses (goddesses of arts), the Graces (goddesses of charm), Helen of Troy (most beautiful mortal woman)

Spouse: No husband, no lovers

Children: No children

Athena was really upset. She **grieved**. Grieve means to feel sad when someone dies. Athena didn't want to forget Pallas. She took her name. She called herself "Pallas Athena." She did this to honor Pallas.

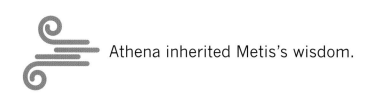

Athena inherited Metis's wisdom.

CHAPTER 2

WISDOM AND WARS

What are Athena's skills and strengths? What gifts did she give to mankind? What are her powers?

Athena was the goddess of wisdom, war, and the arts. She was friendly. She was calm. She didn't anger easily. She fought. She battled. But she needed a good reason to do so. She fought to defend her home. She fought to protect people.

She helped Greek heroes. She used her wisdom to fight wars. She protected Odysseus. She put thoughts in his head. She appeared in his dreams. She changed into a bird. She gave him advice. She guided him safely home. She protected Heracles. She helped him succeed in his tests. Birds attacked Heracles. Athena gave him noisemakers. This scared the birds away.

Athena helped Jason. She built his magical ship. The ship was called the Argo.

Athena was the goddess of the city. She gave mankind many useful things. She invented the **bridle**. A bridle is headgear for a horse. It helps tame horses. Athena invented other farm equipment. She invented rakes, plows, and yokes.

Athena loved heroic endeavors.

All in the Family

Athena didn't have her own children. But she adopted Erichthonius. She took care of him. She wanted to raise him in secret. She put him in a small box. She had three women watch over him. She didn't tell them what was in the box. She forbade them from opening the box. The women opened the box. Erichthonius took the form of a snake. The snake scared the women. Athena punished them. She made them go crazy. They killed themselves. Erichthonius was the son of Hephaestus. Athena wanted to buy weapons from Hephaestus. He tried to marry Athena. Athena said no. She didn't like his limp. She ran away from him. He spilled his seed on earth. This was how Erichthonius was born. Athena made Erichthonius the king of Athens. She protected him.

Athena was the goddess of war strategy.
She caused victories.

She invented ships and **chariots**. Chariots are two-wheeled carts. They're pulled by animals. Her inventions helped mankind. They helped create cities.

Athena gave good advice. She promoted good government. She was the goddess of law and justice. She developed trial by jury. This is when people go to court. The court decides if people are guilty or innocent. She advised Achilles.

She grabbed him by the hair. She warned him. This controlled his anger.

Athena supported arts and crafts. She gave mankind pottery and weaving. She gave them cooking and sewing.

She invented musical instruments. She created the flute. She copied the sound of monsters crying. She looked in a mirror. She saw herself playing. She didn't like her puffed-out cheeks. She didn't like how she looked. The other gods made fun of her. She threw away the flute. She cursed it.

She had many powers. She changed shapes. She changed the shapes of others. She could be invisible. She was strong. She moved quickly. She made storms.

 Athena was the goddess of architects and artists.

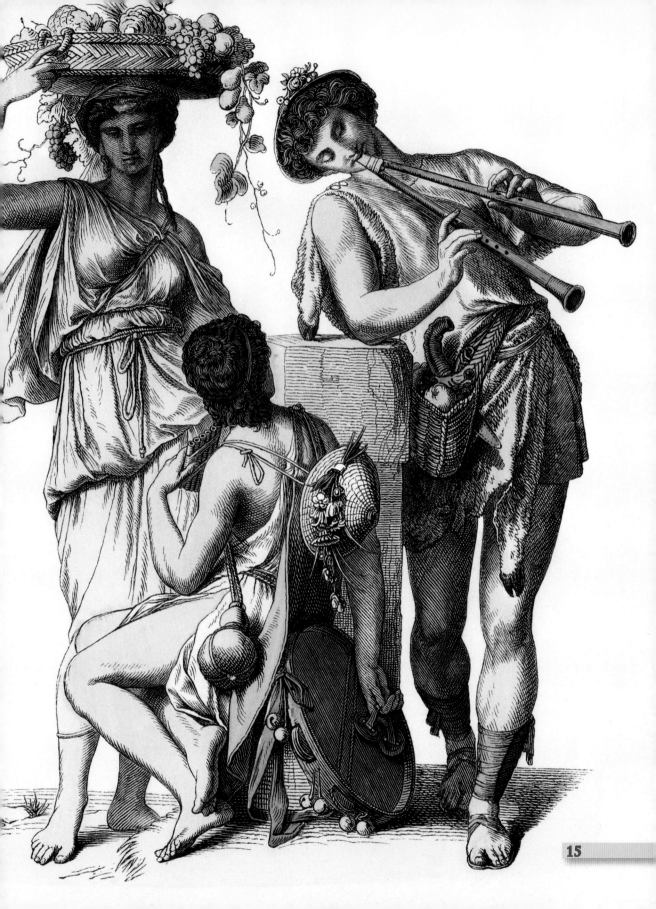

CHAPTER 3

CRUEL AND UNUSUAL PUNISHMENTS

What happened between Athena and Arachne? What happened to Teiresias? What happened to Medusa?

Athena taught Arachne how to weave. Arachne made beautiful rugs. She became a famous weaver. But Arachne became selfish. She said Athena didn't teach her. She said she was better than Athena.

Athena changed into an old woman. She asked Arachne who the best weaver was. Arachne bragged. She said she was the best. Athena changed to her normal self. She challenged Arachne to a weaving contest. Athena wove a picture of **mortals** claiming to be better than gods. Mortals are humans. Arachne wove a picture of the gods' failures. This made Athena mad. Athena cursed Arachne. She turned her into a spider. She made Arachne weave forever.

Athena didn't like mortals breaking rules. No mortal was allowed to see a naked god. Athena took a bath. She was naked. Teiresias watched Athena. This made Athena mad.

Athena didn't like it when mortals mocked the gods.

Real World Connection

Captain Kristen Marie Griest is today's version of a warrior goddess. She graduated from the U.S. Military Academy in 2011. She served in Afghanistan. She was a military police officer. She began Army Ranger training in 2015. She started with 19 other women. This was the first time women were allowed to participate. Women weren't allowed to be in combat. So, this was a special opportunity. Griest failed a couple of times. But she got back to training. She graduated from U.S. Army Ranger School in August 2015. She's one of two women to become an Army Ranger. Army Rangers are an elite fighting force. She's also the Army's first female infantry officer. This allows her to lead soldiers into combat. Griest has broken barriers for female soldiers. She said, "We can handle things physically and mentally on the same level as men."

Athena was often described as "bright-eyed."

Athena blinded Teiresias. But then, she felt bad. She gave him a special gift. She let him understand birds' language. This also meant he could see the future.

Athena didn't like being disrespected. Medusa was a beautiful mortal. Poseidon attacked her in Athena's temple. Poseidon was the god of seas. Athena couldn't punish Poseidon. So, she punished Medusa. She turned her into a monster. Medusa had snakes for hair. She turned anyone who looked at her into stone.

CHAPTER 4

BATTLE GEAR

What is Athena's aegis? What are her weapons? What are her symbols?

Athena helped Perseus kill Medusa. Perseus was a Greek hero. She loaned Perseus a shield. It had a gold surface. Perseus used it as a mirror. He could see Medusa without directly looking at her. Athena guided his sword. Perseus cut off Medusa's head.

Perseus gave Medusa's head to Athena. Athena placed it on her aegis. The aegis was made of animal skin. It had a fringe of snakes. It had scales. With Medusa's head, it was scarier. It inspired fear. It was awful to look at. It killed anyone who saw it. It turned others to stone.

Zeus had given the aegis to Athena. Zeus also let Athena use his thunderbolt. Athena had several weapons. She wore body armor. She had a **lance**. A lance is a spear. She wore a helmet. Her helmet had pictures of a sphinx and two griffins. A sphinx had a human's head. It had a lion's body. A griffin was half-lion. It was half-eagle.

Athena gained power from her battle gear.

Gods need mortals and cities to worship them.

Athena was called the bird goddess. She was connected to owls. She's often pictured with owls. Owls are thought to be wise. They can see at night. They have special eyes. So did Athena. Athena had gray eyes.

Athena gave olive trees to the world. Olive branches mean peace. They're Athena's symbols. Athena preferred peace to war.

Athena fought with Poseidon. They fought over a city. The two gods had a contest. They each gave the city a gift.

Cross-Cultural Connection

Saraswati is a Hindu goddess. She's the goddess of knowledge, music, and arts. She gives humans the power of speech and learning. She's worshipped in India, Nepal, Japan, Vietnam, Indonesia, and Myanmar. She's a beautiful woman. She dresses in pure white. She rides a white swan. She sits on a white lotus. Lotus is a flower. It symbolizes light, knowledge, and truth. White represents purity. Saraswati has four arms. Each arm represents aspects of human personality. One arm represents the mind. One arm represents intelligence. One arm represents imagination. One arm represents ego. Saraswati's four arms hold special items. They hold a book, rosary, water pot, and musical instrument. Saraswati hangs around rivers. Saraswati was the name of a major river of ancient India. Saraswati's name means elegant, flowing, or watery.

The city picked the best gift. The winning god would rule the city.

Poseidon created a horse from sea foam. He gave it to the city. Athena gave an olive tree. Olive trees gave the city wood, oil, and food. Athena won. So, the city was named Athens.

 Athena could see the future. But she couldn't change it.

CHAPTER 5

HELP FROM ATHENA

How was Athena helpful? How did Athena create volcanoes?

There are many myths about Athena.

Athena helped Bellerophon. Bellerophon was a Greek hero. He **slayed** monsters. Slay means to kill. He was asked to kill Chimera. Chimera had a lion's head. It had a goat's body. It had a snake's tail. It breathed fire.

To win, he'd need Pegasus's help. Pegasus was a winged horse. Bellerophon slept in Athena's temple. He needed her advice. Athena gave him a golden bridle. Bellerophon used it. He captured Pegasus. He flew on Pegasus. He choked Chimera. He couldn't have done it without Athena's help.

There was a war between the Giants and the Olympians. Athena fought against Enceladus. Enceladus was a Giant. He was running away from Athena. Athena picked up Sicily. Sicily is an island. She threw the island at Enceladus. The island buried him.

Pegasus's father was the god of the seas, Poseidon.

Enceladus became a volcano. Enceladus would hiss. He'd flash his fiery tongue. He'd breathe. This caused an eruption. Enceladus got restless. He rolled over. This caused earthquakes. This explains why Sicily has Europe's highest active volcano.

Explained By Science

Ancient Greeks didn't know how volcanoes erupted. Science has an explanation. Earth is made up of plates. Plates are huge slabs. The plates fit together like a puzzle. These plates sometimes move. This movement causes earthquakes and volcanoes. Volcanoes are mountains. They open downward to pools of melting rock. Pressure builds up. Gases and rocks shoot up through the opening. This causes eruptions. Eruptions cause tsunamis, floods, and earthquakes. There are three different types of volcanoes: active, dormant, and extinct. Volcanoes are the earth's way of cooling off. They release internal heat and pressure.

One myth about Athena helps explain volcanoes and earthquakes.

Don't anger the gods. Athena had great powers. And she knew how to use them.

DID YOU KNOW?

- Athena fought against Paris, the prince of Troy, in the Trojan War. Athena teamed up with Hera. Paris judged Aphrodite to be the most beautiful woman. Athena took revenge on Paris.

- Athena was close friends with Nike. Nike was the goddess of victory.

- Athena is pictured on the state seal of California.

- The city of Athens honored Athena. Athens was the center of Greek civilization. It was the world's first democracy. Athenians wrote the first plays. Great thinkers like Socrates, Plato, and Aristotle lived in Athens.

- The Parthenon is a famous temple in Athens. It has a large statue of Athena. The statue is made of gold and ivory.

- There were three pure goddesses: Athena, Artemis, and Hestia.

- Ancient Romans worshipped gods. Minerva was the Roman version of Athena. Minerva was the goddess of wisdom. She also sponsored arts, trade, and strategy.

- Athena sewed Hera's wedding veil. Hera married Zeus.

- The gods fought against each other during the Trojan War. Athena's side won. This showed her power. She was the goddess of war victory.

CONSIDER THIS!

TAKE A POSITION Athena had many skills and powers. Which do you think was her best power? Why do you think so? Argue your point with reasons and evidence.

SAY WHAT? Athena was the goddess of war and wisdom. Explain how Athena was a wise warrior. How did she use her wisdom in warfare?

THINK ABOUT IT! Athena was an independent woman. Some say that she was the first "career woman." What does this mean?

LEARN MORE

O'Connor, George. *Athena: Grey-Eyed Goddess*. New York; London: First Second, 2010.

Yim Bridges, Shirin. *Call Me Athena: Greek Goddess of Wisdom*. Foster City, CA: Goosebottom Books, 2014.

GLOSSARY

bridle (BRYE-duhl) special headgear for horses that includes straps and reins

chariots (CHAR-ee-uhts) two-wheeled carts pulled by animals

grieved (GREEVD) mourned and felt sad over a loss

lance (LANS) spear

mortals (MOR-tuhlz) humans

Olympians (uh-LIM-pee-uhnz) rulers of the gods who lived on Mount Olympus

slayed (SLAYD) killed

Titan (TYE-tun) one of the giant gods who ruled before the Olympians

INDEX

A
aegis, 20–21
Arachne, 16–17
Athena
 birth, 6
 family, 4–5, 7
 inventions, 11, 13–14
 and Pallas, 6–9
 powers, 14, 17, 19, 30
 strengths and skills, 10–14, 16
 weapons, 20–21
 who she helped, 10–11, 13, 26–27

B
Bellerophon, 26

C
Chimera, 26

E
earthquakes, 28, 29
Enceladus, 27–28
Erichthonius, 12

M
Medusa, 19, 20
Metis, 4–5, 9

O
olive trees, 22, 24
owls, 22

P
Pallas, 6–9
Pegasus, 26
Perseus, 20
Poseidon, 19, 23–24

T
Teiresias, 17, 19

V
volcanoes, 28, 29

Z
Zeus, 4–6, 9, 21, 30